AF396417

ON DISCOURSE AND THE CURATORIAL

Mick Wilson

Contents

Introduction

8   Why "On the Curatorial"?
       Carolina Rito

On Discourse and the Curatorial
Mick Wilson

24   Incitements to Discourse
38   Taking Turns Talking at Tables
56   Curating/the Curatorial
66   The Discursive Returns
76   To Seminar

WHY "ON THE CURATORIAL"?

Carolina Rito

On the Curatorial is a series of publications that invites respected curators and curatorial scholars to share their insights into "the curatorial." The debate around the curatorial, which was theorized as distinct from "curating," emerged at the turn of the twenty-first century. Now a rather familiar term to many in the curating sphere, the curatorial was introduced with the intention of mapping and exploring the field of aesthetic, discursive, and conceptual activity that emerged from the expansion of curating and, more importantly, the practices beyond the making of exhibitions.

However, why did we need another term to represent and discuss curatorial practices? Curators and academics recognized that there was something more to curating—to the act of making things public, of juxtaposing seemingly unrelated materials, of stimulating the discussion of speculative ideas, of producing new knowledge—than professional skills. In other words, the field of traditional exhibition-making was giving way to a multiplicity of cultural exchanges involving different actors, fields, disciplines, and formats that were underexplored.

The term "curating" fell short in capturing this complexity because it was too tied to exhibitions and their professional skills. Practitioners in the field began to look elsewhere for modes to articulate this new space of cultural production, opening the space for the development of a new conceptual and aesthetic understanding.

Why look at this development now? In the beginning of the twenty–first century, curating theory was dominated by a series of seminal publications on the emerging notion of "the curatorial." Although scattered and not necessarily always connected, these texts laid the groundwork for a debate (2006–13) that is still developing today. Irit Rogoff published "Smuggling – A Curatorial Model" in 2006,[1] followed by Maria Lind's "The Curatorial" in 2009.[2] A couple of years later, Beatrice von Bismarck edited *Cultures of the Curatorial* (2012),[3] and Irit Rogoff and Jean-Paul Martinon coauthored *The Curatorial: A Philosophy of Curating*, published in 2013.[4] Although each text held slightly different ambitions, the number of publications and public events around the term demonstrated the urgency of the emerging conceptualization of the curatorial.

*1   Irit Rogoff, "Smuggling: A Curatorial Model," in *Under Perspectives on Institutional Practice*, ed. Vanessa Joan Müller and Nicolaus Schaffhausen (Cologne: Walther König, 2006), 132–36.

*2   Maria Lind, "The Curatorial," *Artforum*, October 2009, https://www.artforum.com/columns/the-curatorial-192127/.

*3   Beatrice von Bismarck, Jörn Schafaff, and Thomas Weski, eds. *Cultures of the Curatorial* (Berlin: Sternberg Press, 2012).

*4   Jean-Paul Martinon and Irit Rogoff, eds., *The Curatorial: A Philosophy of Curating* (New York: Bloomsbury Academic, 2013).

                                        Carolina Rito

To this day, these texts still form the backbone of the literature on the debates about the differences between the curatorial and curating.

Importantly, the notion of the curatorial sets the scene for the growth of new approaches to the practice of making public material and immaterial cultures, affecting their meanings within and beyond the gallery space. The curatorial highlights the many activities that emerge alongside the creation of exhibitions, constituting a platform for cultural encounters, political assemblages, and social happenings that transcend the initial intention of a curated project. While sharing its beginnings with the expansion of curating, the debate around the curatorial soon took a more independent conceptual dimension, moving away from the centrality of the professional identity of the curator and the representation of themes. The curatorial was, and still is, a manifestation of interest in the aesthetic and political potential of cultural engagement enabled by the act of *making public* and its intrinsically collective nature. The collective nature of the curatorial comprises different degrees of involvement and, therefore, different temporalities of engagement. It includes those who are part of the process of organizing the event, as well as those who find themselves as participants of the constellation of events, materials, and meanings—whether intentionally or not.

Although the intrinsic relationship between curating, as the practice of making exhibitions, and the curatorial was not being questioned when it came to be used, there was a perceived need among curators and academics to explore, both theoretically and practically, how a shift away from the conventional skills and expertise of curators could facilitate a deeper understanding of the aesthetic, philosophical, and political dimensions of these complex, interrelated practices. As Beatrice von Bismarck posited, curating is a constellational activity that brings together disparate elements, including artworks, artifacts, information, people, sites, contexts, resources, and more.[5] The curatorial, in this sense, points to the new cultural, aesthetic, and political affordances of curation as a field whose dynamism gives rise to unplanned situations that take on a life of their own.[6]

It is in the attention paid to the that which was not a planned outcome of the curated event that the curatorial emerges, and where the figure of the curator—or the single author—becomes less relevant. The unplanned outcomes can be seen as a surplus of the event that establishes new rela-tions beyond the curated display of objects (and the meanings attributed to them), or the format of the events, or the topics of the encounters. These interrelationships not only reflect the ecological and environmental dynamism of the curatorial but also give rise to a vast field of knowledge and senses rooted in cultural exchange. How might we, as

*5   Irit Rogoff and Beatrice von Bismarck, "Curating/Curatorial: A Conversation between Irit Rogoff and Beatrice Von Bismarck," in *Cultures of the Curatorial*), 21–30.

*6   Ibid., 25.

                                                     Carolina Rito

organizers, visitors, and participants, make sense of the world *curatorially*? How does the juxtaposition between materials and ideas, artifacts and peoples, create new meanings, worldviews, ecosystems, and narratives? How does the rearticulation of materials enable new imaginaries, politics, and aesthetics in the present?

On the Curatorial invites the authors who introduced the notion of the curatorial and a new generation of curators to take stock of the development of the curatorial as a practice and a philosophical approach. The contributors reflect on the questions: What has happened to the field of curating in the last twenty years? What are the most important and significant developments? How does the curatorial emerge and manifest itself today? And do we need more curatorial tools to engage with the changing landscape of social, political, and climate crises? This series of publications draws on two dimensions of the curatorial: firstly, the specificities of aesthetic, political, and social formations that emerge from the curatorial gesture; and, secondly, the epistemologies enabled by the conditions and relations of the appearance of art and culture in the world. The writers were invited to engage with these two dimensions and relate them to contemporary practices, urgencies, and debates in curating. In this context, "urgencies" points to the ecology of exposures/expositions, in the sense that the curatorial is part of the complex ecological formations of today's crises. This includes the environmental catastrophe, the resurgence of fascist ideologies, the obsolescence of post–World War II humanitarian institutions, and the persisting legacy of colonial violence. The goal is to see the curatorial as an active part of its political context, and to ascertain its role in strengthening the field from where we can continue addressing, questioning, and articulating the world beyond symbolic representation.

In my capacity as a practicing curator and researcher, I have been particularly attentive to the epistemic capacities of the curatorial, and how the latter offers tools that can both investigate and intervene, display and experiment. It is my contention that curatorial research should establish its own conditions for flourishing within the extant infrastructures of the institutions of culture and knowledge production. This would mean embedding curatorial research in the intersection between the cultural sector and the academy, to make use of the resources and skill sets available in both sectors while aiming at something new.

Based on the work I curated as Head of Public Programmes and Research at Nottingham Contemporary (2017–20), I have advanced the proposition that the capabilities of curatorial re-search in the cultural sector could be harnessed to establish a program based on long-term inquiries that activate research questions and create new communities around concerns.[7] This is because research processes require time and collaboration, where audiences and participants could take part in the research process one time as viewers, another time as contributors. A long-term research inquiry,

                                                          Carolina Rito

at the intersection of these sectors, takes its positionality as a forum for speculative and critical engagements, offering creative and unexpected points of entry into the issues at stake. In this way, the cultural sector presents a compelling argument for its role as a site not of representation but of a new site of aesthetic, social, and political formations, operating as a mode of "epistemic praxis."[8]

At Coventry University (UK), where I am professor of creative practice research and chair of the critical practices research strand, we have started a research area—curatorial research—that aims to create space for the intersection of research and curatorial practices. Thought of as a collaboration between the experimentation in cultural production and the investigative nature of research inquiries in academia, the curatorial research cluster probes the investigative capacities of curatorial practices.[9] Together with a transdisciplinary group of colleagues, we unpack the complexities of the politics of exhibitions and their decolonial potential, to provide a look at the ways exposed materials establish epistemic relations between them, its political and aesthetic purchase, as well as its contemporary currency in today's exhibition ecologies.

*7   Carolina Rito, "What Is the Curatorial Doing?" in *Institution as Praxis: New Curatorial Directions for Collaborative Research*, ed. Carolina Rito and Bill Balaskas (Berlin: Sternberg Press, 2020), 44–61.

*8   Carolina Rito and Bill Balaskas, eds., *Institution as Praxis: New Curatorial Directions for Collaborative Research* (Berlin: Sternberg Press, 2020).

*9   See the Curatorial Research site, https://curatorial-research.com/.

We ask questions through curatorial formats such as exhibitions, discussions, workshops, screenings, publications, activism, and more. These formats simultaneously function as methods to advance the research question and as a forum for the collective construction and deconstruction of meanings.

This series aims to extend an invitation to esteemed colleagues to assist us in contemplating these ideas. It is my intention that this series of publications will serve as an important reference point for our studies and practices, and as a catalyst for thought-provoking debates within our research hub in Coventry and beyond. I hope that this series helps shape the direction of debate within the field, be it at artist-run spaces, galleries, off-site exhibitions, museums, research centers, cultural centers, or classrooms, and that it encourages a shift toward new critical perspectives where research and practice converge.

The first volume of the On the Curatorial series is a contribution by Mick Wilson, professor of art, director of doctoral studies at HDK-Valand, University of Gothenburg, and co-chair of the Centre for Art and the Political Imaginary based in the same institution. Wilson has published extensively on contemporary curating. Some of the more distinct coedited volumes are *Thinking Contemporary Curating: Between Contemporary Art and Curatorial Discourses* (2012);[10] *How Institutions Think: Between Contemporary Art and Curatorial Discourse* (2017);[11] and *The Curatorial Conundrum: What to Study? What to Research? What to*

Carolina Rito

Practice? (2016),[12] to name only a few.

In this volume, Wilson returns to one of the central questions of his work, the various manifestations of "discourse" and "the discursive" in curatorial practices, to demonstrate how "the curatorial" has contributed to the rise of the discursive in curating today.[13] It is well known that the proliferation of dialogic formats, from talks to workshops to residencies, has diversified the ways in which curators animate a particular theme in curatorial programming. Wilson makes a clear distinction between discourse "about" exhibitions (i.e., public events about exhibitions, exhibition reviews) and discourse as curatorial events. Going back in time, Wilson reminds us of the role that discourse has played over the years, from the incitement to discourse in the formation of the bourgeois enlightened class during the first Parisian salons to the opening up of exhibition-making to other forms of cultural engagement.

After discussing the various definitions of discourse—and, by extension, its aesthetic and political valences—from philosophy to sociology,

*10   Paul O'Neill, Mick Wilson, and Lucy Steeds, eds., *Thinking Contemporary Curating: Between Contemporary Art and Curatorial Discourses* (New York: Independent Curators International ICI, 2012).

*11   Paul O'Neill, Lucy Steeds, and Mick Wilson, eds., *How Institutions Think: Between Contemporary Art and Curatorial Discourse* (Cambridge, MA: MIT Press, 2017).

*12   Paul O'Neill, Mick Wilson, and Lucy Steeds, eds., *The Curatorial Conundrum: What to Study? What to Research? What to Practice?* (Cambridge, MA: MIT Press, 2016).

*13   Mick Wilson, "Curatorial Moments and Discursive Turns," in *Curating Subjects*, ed. Paul O'Neill and Andreasen Søren (London: Open Editions, 2007), 201–6.

Wilson provides a well-illustrated account of the complexity of discourse in curatorial practice by presenting five instances in which the discursive varies in tones, forms, and textures. These anecdotes serve to highlight the importance of recognizing the discursive not as an exercise in validating the field, but as a way of rehearsing other scenarios and modes of engagement within and beyond language. Concerned that the debate around the curatorial may have become a discourse exercise full of protocols whose only aim is to validate the field, the text emphasizes the importance of seeing the discursive as both a connector between different fields and a disruptive force, capable of generating new possibilities even as it is regulated and used to reinforce social and disciplinary structures.

Carolina Rito

ON DISCOURSE AND THE CURATORIAL

Mick Wilson

The use of the word discursive includes the following consider-ations: first (a technical definition), the movement between subjects without or beyond order; second, a set of discussions marked by their adherence to one or more notions of analytical reason. —Liam Gillick[1]

[I]t is arguably precisely the tension between the generic and the specific that haunts so much curatorial litera-ture. —Gerrie van Noord[2]

*1   Liam Gillick, "Maybe it would be better if we worked in groups of three" (2011), http://www.liamgillick.info/home/texts/maybe-it-would-be-better-to-work-in-groups-of-three.

*2   Gerrie van Noord, "Beyond Hierarchy: Articulating Collaboration," in *Not Going It Alone: Collective Curatorial Curating*, eds. Paul O'Neill, Gerrie van Noor, and Elizabeth Larison (New York: apexart, 2024), 120.

INCITEMENTS TO DISCOURSE

This text began life as a wish to write about curating and the role of discursive events. This is to treat curating not simply as an object of discussion but curating as itself the orchestration of discussion. The topic is prompted by recurrent claims that curatorial practice hosts and enables discursive encounters in an open-ended and capacious manner.[3] I have often encountered these claims while working with curators engaged in research both within and beyond doctoral training.[4] Maria Lind's influential early formulation of the curatorial as "a way of linking objects, images, processes, people, locations, histories, and discourses in physical space" positions discourse as an integral element of curating practice and of the curatorial.[5] This is not discourse as a secondary commentary superimposed upon a practice of curating that unfolds in some extra-discursive register, but rather discursivity as a curatorial mode in its own right.

The ascendancy of the discursive—a term that is further elaborated below—in curating is conditioned by two major shifts. On the one hand,

*3   Okwui Enzewor's 2002 Documenta 11 is generally accepted as a key moment in explicitly centering discursive operations as integral to curatorial practice, i.e., as substantive curatorial production that is not ancillary or supplemental to exhibition. His 2002 contribution "The Black Box" to the *Documenta11_Platform 5: Exhibition, Catalogue* foregrounded the move "outside the domain of the gallery space to that of the discursive" (Stuttgart: Hatje Cantz, 2002), 42. He also asserted that "the discursive drive of Documenta 11 will never see its conclusion in the spectacular spaces filled with art projects that the exhibition offers to visitors to Kassel" (42). This leads to: "The public sphere of the exhibition gesture… is rearticulated here as a new understanding in the domain of the discursive rather than the museological" (54).

there is the increase in discursive production attendant upon a massively expanded field of curatorial practices, both in the sheer volume of projects and in the range of formats other than exhibition making. These developments are typically located in the 1980s and 1990s and identified, inter alia, with the global dissemination of the biennial form and the emergence of many new curatorial training programs.[6] On the other hand, a complementary construct has emerged: the curatorial, which Lind and others have elaborated as a way of signaling the epistemological potentials of curating beyond its

*4   The theme of curating as an enabler of discursive openness and breadth emerges quite often in the context of doctoral research on curating and the curatorial, echoing the epistemological stakes of Enzewor's claims on discursivity. Instances include Alexandra C. M. Ross's *Continuous Curatorial Conversations: An Exploration of the Role of Conversation within the Writing of a Supplementary History of the Curatorial* (2014), Anne Julie Arnfred's doctoral dissertation *Curating Situated Practices: Entanglements In-Between Art, Academia, and Lived Experiences* at (2024, Roskilde University, Roskilde), indicating the persistence of this theme over a decade and also evidencing very different degrees of criticality in the construction of specifically curatorial conversations and discursive practices. An important development in this context is Stéphanie Bertrand's doctoral dissertation *Curating Content: Inclusion, Transparency and Mediation in Contemporary Curatorial Practice* (2019, Aristotle University, Thessaloniki) where she advances a critique of "contemporary curating's current iterative discourse" (231); its "common discursive roundabouts" (222); and its "discursive stalemate" (231). Bertrand later developed her thesis work into the monograph *Contemporary Curating, Artistic Reference and Public Reception: Reconsidering Inclusion, Transparency and Mediation in Exhibition Making Practice* (London and New York: Routledge, 2022).

*5   Maria Lind, "The Curatorial," *Artforum*, October 2009, 109.

*6   See Paul O'Neill, *The Culture of Curating and the Curating of Culture(s)* (Cambridge, MA: MIT Press, 2012); and Terry Smith, *Thinking Contemporary Curating* (New York: Independent Curators International, 2015).

                                                    Mick Wilson

operational dimensions. This couplet of "curating/
the curatorial" is considered further below; however,
for now it suffices to note that claims for curating's
capacity to organize creative discursive encounters
are connected to claims for the curatorial's potential to foster and enable new forms of knowledge
making.

I had originally intended to write about the
tensions surrounding discursive production in the
domain of curating and the different ways in which
the discursive is proposed as constitutive or oper-
ative for the curatorial. In executing the task other
problems heaved into view. One was the question
of the discursive's definite character and the basic
questions of how language and language acts are
to be construed. David Abram, in his influential *The
Spell of the Sensuous*, argues eloquently that: "Every
attempt to definitively say what language is is subject to a curious limitation. For the only medium with
which we can define language is language itself. We
are therefore unable to circumscribe the whole of
language within our definition."[7] Complicating things
further, the breadth of figures and terms of discursivity such as conversation, discourse, dialogue, and
the dialogical, not only within the contemporary art
but also across the humanities and social and psychological sciences, means that there is significant
divergence in the ways in which language events are
differentiated. This latitude of meaning and usage

*7　David Abram, *The Spell of the Sensuous: Perception and
Language in a More-than-Human World* (New York: Vintage,
1996), 52

requires a clarification of terminology, and so I begin with a thoroughly provisional elaboration of the term "discursive."

The discursive is used here to indicate language use in both its oral and textual forms and without reference to a specific genre. It is, for now, implicitly a matter of human language while questions of the more-than- and the other-than-human are deferred. There are two central aspects to the discursive: (i) it indicates the sociomateriality[8] of the language act (linking ideas of language as code, system, or abstract order of referentiality to concrete, situated instances of production where language use is not seen as reducible to mere information exchange); (ii) it identifies language events as situated within a wider nexus of processes and actors and as such not simply isolated or self-sufficient occasions of meaning-making. Importantly, this understanding of the discursive rejects the gloss offered by Liam Gillick and cited at the head of this essay. The discursive is not necessarily a matter of the subject and intersubjectivity, nor does it entail by default a principle of analytical reason.

"Discourse" and the "discursive" derive etymologically from the Latin *discursus*, which indicates a running back and forth. This movement to and fro is an important aspect of the sense of discursivity as a dynamic and multiple field of interoperation. This might be contrasted with the tendency

*8   It may be helpful to note that the term "sociomaterial density" is used above to emphasize that materiality is not simply physical thing-ness.

                                                      Mick Wilson

to use the term discourse to signal the regularities and recurrent forms of the sayable that characterize specific domains of discursive production. Part of the richness of these terms is the way in which they operate in subtle variation with each other, complemented by a wider spectrum of concepts such as conversation, dialogue, and the dialogical, which indicate dynamics of language exchange and circulation or deploy images of language exchange as a metaphor of reasoning, as in the case of dialectic.[9]

*9   The Latin verb *discurrere*, typically glossed as meaning "to run about," and its nominal form *discursus* ("a running about"), are part of the etymology of discursive and discourse. In the development of these terms and the transfer from Latin to French and subsequently to 16th-century English, it is notable that the terms were not used to mark a distinction between spoken and written language. It is also notable that they for a time retained the sense of a running to and fro, and even of rambling about or covering many topics. In Late Latin, *discursus* was correlated with the image of conversation and of people talking together, while in Medieval Latin, *discursus* was linked to reasoning and argument. The term conversation follows a different etymology that pivots on the Latin *versare*, a term of turning built upon *vertere*, meaning to turn, giving *con-versare* the meaning of turning with or turning together. It may help to think here of terms in English such as re-verse, ad-verse, per-verse, in-verse, and con-version, which also draw upon this etymological development of *versare*. From the Latin *conversari*, meaning "keep company with," emerged the late Middle English sense of "live among, be familiar with," and eventually the current sense of "converse," as in to talk together, becomes widely established in English in the early 17th century. "Dialectic" flows along a different line of development, beginning with the Greek term *diagelesthai*, meaning to talk together. We should note here that "dialogue" came to modern European languages from Greek (the conjunction of *dia-*, meaning through, and *-logos*, indicating word, speech, and reason). The key semantic themes that appear across all of these terms are: (i) movement and (ii) plurality. The figures of the discursive are figures that move and multiply, in contrast to the fixed and the unitary. This might be understood in contrast to those figures of reason that posit it as singular, univocal, and haunted by the threat of nullity posed by contradiction and that use of language that might speak against itself.

In summary, then, the discursive is a way of naming the situated usage of language, emphasizing that this usage cannot be reduced to an understanding of language exclusively as a code or system of referentiality.[10] Discursivity is therefore not restricted to the practice of argument and debate nor to the principle of reason.

I have begun with this necessarily abstract formulation so as to avoid committing on the specific agencies at work in the event of language production such as the speaker/writer (the subject), questions of intentionality, and so forth. (Note that attending to human language is not a matter of positing human agency as definitive but rather a matter of attending to an occasion and condition of language production.) The term "usage" here does not necessarily mean an operation that is already fully subordinated to an intended outcome or goal. It simply indicates the apparent referential tendency of a given instance of language production.[11] My gloss of discursivity is informed by a broad shift in scholarship, from the 1960s onward and across many disciplines, which reprioritized rhetorical

*10   Asserting that language usage is irreducible to specifying a code or a referential system entails seeing the production of language as a material practice constrained and enabled by conditions and processes that are not reducible to acts of symbolic encoding and decoding or to acts of reference. This formulation might be seen as a reversal of the infamous Derridian motto "nothing outside the text" (*il n'y a pas de hors-texte*) by the counterpoint of asserting "language always more than, other than language." The proposition is that in describing language we must attend to more than language, even though what we can attend to may seem somehow constrained to what can be languaged.

                                                  Mick Wilson

analysis and inflected the earlier linguistic turn in philosophy through a consideration of the materiality and concrete situatedness of speaking, writing, and all manner of language production. This formulation of the discursive will be modified as the text proceeds.

This brings us, then, to the space of the curatorial as—in Lind's formulation—an assemblage of discourse and other processes and things unfolding in physical space. We may oppose Lind's stance to modernism's suspicion of discursive imposition upon an artwork, based on the faith in its aesthetic self-sufficiency. Given the familiar suspicions of the excesses of artspeak and of curating's rhetorics,

*11 Gustav Bergmann is generally credited with initiating the use of the term "linguistic turn" to indicate "the linguistic turn Wittgenstein initiated in the *Tractatus*," pointing to the logical positivists as "philosophers through language; they philosophize by means of it. But then, everybody who speaks uses language as a means or tool. The point is that the positivists, newly conscious of it, use it in a new way. The novelty is I believe radical." Gustav Bergmann "Logical Positivism, Language and the Reconstruction of Metaphysics," *Rivista Critica di Storia della Filosofia* 8, no. 4 (July–August 1953): 453–81. I am using the term here more expansively to refer not simply to the linguistic projects of the logical positivists and analytic philosophy but to the broader reorientation among key thinkers in other traditions to attend to language as both a condition of possibility and constraint for philosophical projects. This goes beyond conceptual clarification of terms and extends to such projects as the Foucauldian analysis of discursive formations and Derrida's *Of Grammatology*. The current form of inheritance of these diverse projects seems to be in: (i) the attempt to build a materialist account of language; (ii) the attempt to describe and theorize language as something more/other than the scene of intersubjectivity and the production of "the subject"; (iii) the attempt to describe and theorize language so as to address questions of representation/reference while taking account of postrepresentational critiques of represenationalism; and (iv) the attempt to assimilate developments in "large language models" to accounts of language and language development.

my original intention was to consider the fault lines and tensions in the different ways that the discursive is deployed within curatorial production. Attempting to address some of these issues in an essay on "Curatorial Moments and Discursive Turns" published almost two decades ago, I identified an "ambivalence… as to the value of the discursive." I indicated then how discursive production is seen as valuable when it is "open" but also at risk of becoming "excessive or unbounded."[12]

The recent turn to the discursive resonates with historical scholarship on the Salons of the French Royal Academy of Painting and Sculpture from the 1730s to the 1750s, a period that marked the early development of the modern exhibitionary system. In an important essay written some twenty years ago, William Ray describes the role of these Salons in "the formation of the discursive citizen."[13] Ray argues that these occasions of exhibition became "a crucible for the modern ideology of individualism and the discursive activity it entails."

*12 Mick Wilson, "Curatorial Moments and Discursive Turns," in *Curating Subjects*, ed. P. O'Neill (London: Open Editions, 2007), 201–6. More recently, Stéphanie Bertrand has identified another tension in curating's valuation of the discursive, proposing that contemporary curating converges on "openness, dissensus, processuality, experimentation, emergence and indeterminacy" and "against closure, fixity and definiteness" as its discursive values. Stéphanie Bertrand, *Contemporary Curating, Artistic Reference and Public Reception: Reconsidering Inclusion, Transparency and Mediation in Exhibition Making Practice* (London and New York: Routledge, 2022), 100.

*13 William Ray, "Talking about Art: The French Royal Academy Salons and the Formation of the Discursive Citizen," *Eighteenth-Century Studies* 37, no. 4, Artistic Interactions (Summer 2004): 527–52.

Mick Wilson

The Salons accomplished this by drawing viewers "into discursive engagement" and identification with "consensual forms of authority out of which both the prestige of public opinion and the ideal of the self-expressive individual would ultimately blossom." Though a little caution toward the teleological tendency in this analysis is warranted, it is hard not to be struck by Ray's most important claim:

> The most fundamental political consequences of the early art exhibit are not to be found in the way it represents and thus exercises social concern around specific historical events, ideals, styles, or aesthetic doctrines, but rather in the way it instigates discursive involvement in the people it attracts, implicating their particular identities in the acquisition of shared habits of public discussion, and thus paving the way for the modern era's outspoken, self-regulating citizen.[14]

Ray identifies the civilizing or disciplining role of the exhibition in its incitement to discourse, theorizing it as a discursive apparatus—an occasion for the production of discourse by amateurs as a means of inscribing themselves into an emergent bourgeois social order—rather than as an apparatus of visibility or representation. In contrast, Tony Bennet's highly influential analysis of the nineteenth-century public museum—a form that later emerges in a line of

*14   Op. cit. 544.

genealogical descent from the eighteenth-century Salons—foregrounds visibility in the sense of the scopic organization of attention as the primary disciplinary register, and not discursivity as such.[15]

In the twenty-first century, the discursivity of contemporary curating practices, most particularly within the contemporary art space, and the solic-itation of all manner of conversational encounter in and around the exhibition (and other formats of production) are not typically or primarily seeking to cultivate a discourse in direct response to visual dis-plays. Indeed, the pursuit of direct correspondences between the seeable and the sayable is much more attenuated in the contemporary curatorial incite-ment to discourse than, say, in the earlier discourses of art criticism, which arguably have been displaced by the recent ascendance of curating and the curator.[16]

The newfound prominence of all manner of discursive formats—from public program seminars and symposia to thematically structured residen-cies to complex research trajectories and various

*15   Tony Bennett, *The Birth of the Museum: History, Theory, Politics* (London & New York: Routledge, 1995).

*16   Liam Gillick observed that criticism "has become either a thing of record, or a thing of speculation whereas the curatorial voice has become the parallel critical voice to the artist that contributes a parallel discourse." Liam Gillick as quoted by Saskia Bos in her "Towards a Scenario: Debate with Liam Gillick," the *De Appel Reader No. 1: Modernity Today: Contributions to a Topical Artistic Discourse* (Amsterdam: De Apple, 2004), 7. Paul O'Neill, citing Gillick, reframed this as "the neocritical curator has usurped the evacuated place of the critic," also in his "The Curatorial Turn: From Practice to Discourse," in *The Biennial Reader*, ed. Elena Filipovic et al. (Berlin: Hatje Cantz, 2010), 241.

                                                             Mick Wilson

ambitious publishing programs—indicates an impulse to promote discursive production in ways that go far beyond thematizing the visible in displayed works. These formats operate in ways no longer adequately described in the analysis of the scopic discipline of the nineteenth-century museum. However, as has on occasion been remarked, there are other forms of discipline at work in the cultivation of discursive assembly and conversational exchange as curatorial and artistic strategies.[17] Ray's historical interpretation has informed my choice of topic and suggested further questions in relation to contemporary practices: How does the incitement to discourse as an aspect of contemporary curating and artistic practice sit in relation to the civilizing imperative as described by Ray and Bennet in the genealogy of the exhibitionary complex and the museum? Is this a matter of a persistent incitement to discourse within the exhibitionary process that predates the 1990s and the rise of the curatorial, or are we witnessing a discontinuous and discrete emergence of a different regime?

Rather than address these questions head on, in what follows I provide concrete instances of the discursive through a series of anecdotal, conversational exchanges. I opt for this more circuitous

*17   Here I am including both the discursive events organized around or as supplement to the exhibition, residency, artwork, or other project format, and the the discursive events that are in themselves the primary curatorial and artistic production. These discursive events extend far beyond the verbal elaboration of visual display or the attempt to give verbal form to visual experience or judgments of taste.

approach out of caution at the totalizing gestures that attach to the framing of such questions, a suspicion of the foundational moves in setting these up, and a caution at *definitively* saying "what language is." The anecdotes also serve as a corrective to the earlier account of the discursive turn cited above. I then explore the discursive operations at work in the production of the curatorial field, specifically in the rhetorical strategies around the thematic couplet "curating/the curatorial." The closing section of the essay turns to a discussion of a specific work within a curatorial project that not only operates across multiple registers but seeks to rearticulate the discursive beyond the existing paradigm. This digressive circuit sets up the possibility of a re-specification of the initial program of inquiry and a reimagining of curating and discursivity. I am reaching for a materialist articulation of discourse that requires us to think materiality beyond simply the paradigm of the discretely localizable physical thing.

TAKING TURNS
TALKING AT TABLES

It is a Saturday evening. I am gathered with some of my siblings and their partners around a restaurant table in Dublin. In age, we range from early forties to early sixties; we are four from a larger set of seven siblings, accompanied by two more, brave partners who have joined a clan meeting of their notoriously voluble in-laws. It is not so often that we gather in this kind of social constellation. There is no specific occasion to meet, just the contingent circumstance that we each happen to be in our hometown at the same time and not otherwise committed. We have been placed in a dark corner of the restaurant, in the basement near the kitchen entrance, possibly because the waiter already anticipates that ours will be a tricky table of jostling and giddy demand.

Our conversations are immediately multiple and crossing in their purposes. While an elder brother attempts to amuse and joke with the waiter about a recommended wine—What side of the valley? How high on the slope? What day of the week picked?—a younger sister mocks him for imposing his overused lines on the put-upon restaurant staff. Another sister attempts to provide unasked-for reassurance to the waiter, qualifying her brother's faltering jokes with a gently dismissive "Ahh, don't mind him. He thinks he's funny. Just serve the rest of us and we'll take care of him for you." Meanwhile, the remaining trio at the table try to work out the last occasion we had reason to meet up in this particular grouping: "It's been quite a while. Has something happened?" The conversation rocks along, the turn-taking boisterous and seemingly arbitrary, people switching in and out of different thematic strands—"No, I think she left that job now…"/"Don't you think they need to find an alternative to direct provision in asylum cases?"/"I'm not sure they still make those parts anymore…"/"Did you say you're going to Poland tomorrow?"/"Is he still going on about the wine?" Occasionally, someone in the company expresses a little dismay at "not being able to get a word in edgeways." However, when the question of dessert arises, all speakers converge upon it. We respond in neat, quick turns to our eminently patient and skilled waiter-cum-secret-moderator of our discussions.

It is the following Monday morning. I am now seated amid another arrangement of tables, distributed not in a restaurant this time, but in a large museum hall. I am among not family intimates but rather a mixture of familiar and newer colleagues, friends acquired through years of collaborative work and some new faces, too. The occasion of our encounter is a meeting over two days to discuss the implementation of a new long-term research project. We have arrived in the space as a large group of some forty or more people, ranging in age from late twenties to early sixties. Without individually assigned seating, we each must position ourselves around the room. We take up our places slowly at first, a little hesitant in stationing ourselves, as if our seating choices might betray our strategic ambition and intentions. Such calculations that avow a means-ends rationale of encounter seem contrary to the informal, convivial networking spirit of the meeting. There is just the risk that these gambits

Mick Wilson

might lack the requisite subtlety.

We have been summoned to attention now by the guest moderator, who takes us through the protocols of the conversational encounter about to unfold. We are encouraged to use the name-tag stickers provided to identify ourselves for colleagues. We are told that we can add information about our institutional affiliation and preferred pronouns. The convenor rehearses their role in the meeting and gives a short account of their identity and life-narrative. They then lay out the rules of the conversation: the need to actively listen and not to speak over each other, the importance of maintaining a certain horizontality so that our different institutional roles do not determine or restrict our capacities to contribute to the discussion, and several more practical behavioral and technical desiderata. The conversations begin at each table, and the table paper coverings are marked up with simple quick drawings and notes that act as traces of our discussions as the morning progresses. After two hours or so, we are reluctantly drawn back to converge our attention upon our convenor, who, having made several verbal and gestural bids to get the room's full focus, now seems a little irked at not getting it sooner, achieving this finally only via the intervention of the meeting's formal host and their more compelling call to order.

These two scenes of conversational encounter operate in different registers, moving from obligations of the sib to obligations of the job, from the informal formulas of kin sociality to the formulaic

informalities of workplace interactions, and from
the substantially unchosen relations of family to the
substantially unchosen relations of employment.
These anecdotes propose a contrast between
two different regulatory styles of conversational
encounter. These lead us to a third conversational
scenario that centers the figure of the one-to-one
encounter rather than the crowded table and brings
a different schema of regulation into view through
the *mise-en-scène* of an artist's conversation piece.

I am sitting in a museum, elegantly draped in a
scarlet-red gown that pools around my feet, reveal-
ing only my face and hands. I am well practiced in
this discipline of holding my body on public display
for long stretches of time. I exercise a mental and
physical discipline that quiets and guides my inner
voice to flow smoothly, patiently measured in the
willed, slow, purposive unfolding of consummate
self-possession. I sit at the table. I sit for many
days. I am in my seventies; those who come to see
me range in age from their teens to their nineties.
Those gathered around me watch carefully, watch-
ing my intent with intent. I have, with institutional
ventriloquism, set up an invitation in the form of an
instruction: "Sit silently with the artist for a duration
of your choosing." They come and they sit with
me. We look to each other. Each of them looks with
different mood or anticipation, their eyes meeting
mine, refocusing with rising or falling inhibition. We
do not speak. Though our encounters are much
spoken about, still, we do not speak. Sometimes, as
my temporary cohabitor moves to leave the table,

                                              Mick Wilson

ending their turn and just before another in the waiting queue assumes their place, they will say, perhaps timidly, perhaps tearfully, perhaps joyfully, a quiet "thank you."[18]

Here, again, there is a different regulatory style at work in setting up and maintaining the conditions of a conversational encounter. The requirement to come into physical proximity and to give and receive corporeal address, to look to each other, sets up a conversational mode of encounter not with immediate verbal exchange, but rather an exchange of silences. This brings us again to the sociomaterial densities, the bodily attunement and address that texture and are textured by conversation. The speech moment is deferred or repressed, subjugated to the imperative to be silent (complementary to the characteristic imperative to speak in discursive encounters) and give attention to our presence together in the shared time and space that are gathered in this theater of display. There are other nonverbal channels and registers of interaction in play. These are perhaps more pronounced because the familiar words are left unpronounced. The conceit of the work appears to be that, in the temporary bracketing-out of speaking from the conversational encounter, another form of authentic engagement becomes possible. This is an encounter with our integral corporeal and psychological presence, an imaginary encounter that seems to

*18   Marina Abramović. *The Artist Is Present*, 2009, https://www.moma.org/audio/playlist/243/3133.

be obscured by the banal and noisy chitchat of everyday speaking encounters. Of course, the entire theater of this museum display is permeated, delimited, and inscribed by language acts; it is just that the specific distribution of language and of speaking is here orchestrated to create a focal point in the unspoken.

These three scenes are not proposed as instances of curating or the curatorial, although the second and third stories are located within a contemporary art setting. Rather, they are the means of pointing to the multiplicity of conversational forms and styles, signaling the tangle of the social body threaded through the exchange of utterance and silence.[19] Hopefully, these scenes illustrate something of the different ways in which the utterances/silences accumulating in such encounters react, counteract, and retroact upon each other, instantiating the conversational without reducing it to the textual or producing an abstracted, ideal paradigm of *the* conversation.

I bring a fourth scene of conversation into play to further elaborate what is at stake in the sociomaterial density of conversation and in holding out for the mutual irreducibility of the conversational and the textual. Although it is designated as a "curated conversation," it is not a scene in the domain of contemporary art, nor is it an instance of curating. It is a staged encounter of four anthropologists

*19   It is not incidental that the different codes of conduct shaping these encounters might hint at their inflection by questions of class, etiquette, and bodily discipline.

                                                           Mick Wilson

coming together to discuss the conundrum of the materiality of language, taken from a source I came upon while looking at how different disciplines approach this thorny question and try to see beyond the analogy between language event and discrete, physical thing. Meeting in a hotel room in Chicago, on the edges of the American Anthropological Association annual conference, these scholars hold a conversation recorded for the purpose of transcription and eventual publication under the title "Curated Conversation: 'Materiality: It's the Stuff!'"[20] The editors Jillian Cavanaugh and Shalini Shankar had invited Webb Keane and Michael Silverstein, two of the four distinguished anthropologists mentioned above, to engage in a conversation about language, materiality, and semiotics. The duo responded to questions already emailed in advance, which included: "Why materiality now?"[21] and "What remains to be said about the relationship between the semiotic and the material?"[22]

There is a giddy, cascading reflexivity to this conversation that is signaled in the transcript by the speakers' overlapping utterances, their playful citations and moments of laughter, and the friendly jostling to mobilize different authors' names and set thematics in play, as can be seen in the following extract:

*20 Webb Keane and Michael Silverstein, "Curated Conversation: 'Materiality: It's the Stuff!'" in *Language and Materiality: Ethnographic and Theoretical Explorations*, ed. Jillian Cavanaugh and Shalini Shankar (Cambrdge, UK, and New York: Cambridge University Press, 2017), 29–40.

*21 Keane and Silverstein, "Curated Conversation," 29.

*22 Keane and Silverstein, "Curated Conversation," 31.

MS   One can even go back further and look at someone like McLuhan, who was very influential in his day... He was really somebody who wanted to épater le bourgeois [shock the middle class] but he never got beyond the notion of a kind of unanalyzable functionality of stuff, of things as instruments.
WK   Right, right.
MS   Everything was an instrument. The prosthesis human
WK   A prosthesis, and therefore, as indeed, at least, some of the minor Latourians
MS   Minor Latourians, I like that [laughs]
WK   In the sense that, to the extent that they are
MS   You mean like an off-vintage? [laughter] He's not Château Latour, he's not the Bordeaux family. He's Louis Latour, the Burgundy family, so it's much less prestigious wines.
WK   To the extent that you treat material things as extensions, in McLuhan's sense, or as having agency with which they are endowed by virtue of that kind of extensionality, then to that extent it invites you to dematerialize them once again by finding the ultimate locus, the source of that agency in some kind of will, or some kind of agentive project

   Mick Wilson

which, for which itself there is no material account.

The playful banter is also integral to the elaboration of different ways of attending to the materiality of language. The following passage illustrates how the conversational dynamic, with its interacting layers of aural and social interactivity, seems to condition the arc of ideation:

> MS   Yeah, yeah. But again, all these people in a really interesting way come up against precisely… the problem… flagged, or denoted by the rubric of "materiality." In all of its forms, its quiddity. Wonderful word! My teacher Quine used to use it all the time.
>
> WK   That's overdeterministic, Jakobson would be the first to note.
>
> MS   What?
>
> WK   Quine's quiddity.
>
> MS   Yes, yes, yes absolutely. The quiddity of Quine.
>
> WK   It's the Jakobsonian point being that the materiality of poetics is the materiality of language.

This passage, with its wordplay and quickfire switching from affirmation ("Yeah, yeah") to seeming negation ("That's overdeterministic") and back to an emphatic and recuperative avowal ("Yes, yes, yes absolutely"), is key to the development of a position on what attending to the materiality of language entails. This is further elaborated later in the exchange:

WK   Right. So it seems to me that two
points about language and materiality
point to different directions in this
relationship or this dialectic. One is, as
Jakobson made clear half a century
ago, that language is itself an object
of experience, that poetics only exist
by virtue of people's response to the
actual sensual experience of language.
So, that language is not something you
go through to get to something else,
whether that be structures of the mind
or that be propositional content, but
that it also has palpable qualities in its
own right, which are not, as it were,
immaterial.
MS   Textual qualities.
WK   Textual qualities. So, that's the
first point, that I think is abundantly
clear. The second is the role that
language plays in the processes of
typification or objectification, not in
the materialization sense of the word
objectification, but in the conceptualization. That is to say the role that
language plays in the ongoing production of awareness and particularly,
I think of interest to us, of sociological
awareness or sociopolitical awareness.

                                    Mick Wilson

This provisional construction of the dialectic of materiality and language produces a series of recursive moments where the conversation does what it thematizes. As with many processes of recursion and self-reference, a space of potential paradox and tension opens up in the conversation and in the transcription. This is especially palpable around the unsettled articulations of the material, the textual, and the conversational. For example, in outlining the rationale, nature, and fate of the transcribed conversation, the instigators propose a contrast of text and conversation that seems to unsettle the concept of materiality in play:

> The "curated conversation" is also a materialized trace of a fleeting interaction that was multiply transformed as it was captured in a digital audio-recording, transcribed, and edited to enhance its readability—making it more textlike and less like an interaction (with all the requisite interruptions, repairs, overlaps, and humorous asides, such as the comment by Silverstein we took as the title, "Materiality: It's the Stuff!"). We have strived to preserve some of its interactive nature as an unfolding conversation, balanced against the needs of readers to be able to encounter it as a text on the page.[23]

*23   Keane and Silverstein, "Curated Conversation," 29.

Keane and Silverstein affirm the materiality of language as "an object of experience" and correlate this with its textual quality, which proceeds from "the actual sensual experience of language."[24] The textual quality has to do with language's "palpable qualities in its own right."[25] Cavanaugh and Shankar designate the transcription, in which these expressions appear, as a "materialized trace" of a "fleeting interaction" and as becoming less conversational and more textlike in being "edited to enhance its readability," which makes it "less like an interaction."[26] There is an emergent tension between the textual and the conversational; in one reading (Keane and Silverstein's) the notion of the textual seems to encompass the actual sensuous experience of language in conversation, whereas in another reading (Cavanaugh and Shankar's), conversation becomes more textlike through losing some of its "interactive" nature. This tension is not simply a reprise of the familiar orality/textuality contrast. It points to the ambivalences of the materiality of language, how the disparity between interactive conversation and published transcription becomes a contrast between degrees of materiality. In other words, the edited transcription is more thingly than the conversation.

*24   Keane and Silverstein, "Curated Conversation," 38.

*25   Keane and Silverstein, "Curated Conversation," 38.

*26   Jillian Cavanaugh and Shalini Shankar, "Toward a Theory of Language Materiality: An Introduction," in *Language and Materiality*, 17.

Mick Wilson

We can, no doubt, concur with Cavanaugh and Shankar when they assert that "materiality is provocative precisely because of the many ways it has been and continues to be conceptualized."[27] The volume in which this transcribed conversation appears announces in its introduction that "to regard linguistic practices… as immaterial is to miss not only how language interacts with physical objects, environments, and forces but also to elide the material nature of linguistic practice itself—its sounds, shape, and material presences."[28] This wish to attend to the materiality of language seems to be troubled by an ambiguity in the requisite density of what is properly material. The figure of materiality in play seems in part to be indebted to images of language's thingly persistence in the form of recording and transcription.

I've brought these four scenarios of conversation into play in my attempt to explore the conjunction of curating and discursivity, seeking to identify the tensions in the deployment of discursivity as curatorial practice. I have sat down to a table to do just this, addressing my body to a laptop while in the imagined company of several dialogue partners: my editor, my students, my colleagues, my friends, and future readers yet more remote. As I do so, I can hear this imagined readership protest.

*27   Cavanaugh and Shankar, "Toward a Theory of Language Materiality: An Introduction," 2.

*28   Cavanaugh and Shankar, "Toward a Theory of Language Materiality: An Introduction," 2.

They ask: Why have you chosen to begin with this somewhat arbitrary set of anecdotes and narrative scenes of conversation rather than describe specific instances of curatorial practice? They push back at me, saying: you seem to be intent on writing away from the scene of curatorial practice as such and attend only to talk about talk. You retreat from the things in question to merely indulge your own questioning, becoming ever more remote from the things themselves. By what right do you do this? According to what regime of good sense can you claim this digressive and indirect pathway correct?

I gather myself to respond and declare that I digress in order to seek in good faith a correct pathway. These stories are introduced as corrective devices that elaborate and problematize the terms already set in play on the discursive side of this conjunction: the conversational, the textual, language, and so forth. But, now here I am describing the scene of my writing as it plays out in my imagination, sitting down to write and getting caught up in one more scenario of discursive encounter. This description seems to default to those familiar contrasts of presence and absence, of writing and orality and all those other imaginaries that I was supposed to have been disabused of decades ago by the great flurry of the late twentieth-century Franco-American theory transfers and authorial corpses. Yet, nonetheless, here I am imagining myself at the table, writing to you in a conversation of some kind and trying to persuade you that there is something correct about this. Although my

                                        Mick Wilson

gambit was that these short narratives of conversation would work to correct something, they seem themselves also in need of correction. But why all this fuss and talk of correction?

The need for correction proceeds from my earlier essay mentioned above, an essay that tried to identify and problematize the "discursive turn" and that was produced within a wider debate on the specificity of curating and the curatorial field just at the threshold of what would become a prolific debate on "the curatorial." That essay began by noting a recurrent ambivalence within curatorial discourse and the contemporary art field as to its valuation of the discursive—"just talk"—while also itemizing a range of art practices that self-consciously pivot on forms of language production, conversation, and discussion. It also tracked the trope of "dialogue" as a metaphor employed to describe the interaction of works of art as used both in art-historical narrative and in exhibition making. Along the way, the essay also made use of an imagined reader, an imaginary dialogue partner to challenge my authorial shtick: "It may be countered that the metaphor of art as a conversation has a pervasive presence in art commentary throughout modernity, and that modernism's dependence upon an integral strand of critical discourses makes this notion of a discursive turn somewhat overblown."[29] The rejoinder to my staged interlocutor came easy, of course: "However, it may in turn be argued that precisely the ways in

*29   Wilson, "Curatorial Moments and Discursive Turns," 208.

which the metaphor of 'the conversation of culture' is being actualised or literalised in recent practices is what marks a significant re-orientation."[30]

These images of specific encounters are used to figure conversation rather than construct a fully abstracted concept or categorical definition.[31] The scenes are proposed as a corrective to the ways in which my earlier essay cursorily gathered the discursive, the linguistic, the conversational, the dialogical, and a few other forking constructs and herded them along one broad—and, as it now appears, incorrect—path. The earlier text dealt with these under the heading of "the discursive" without putting much time into the differences between these formats and modes. Still, its framing of the discursive enabled an exploration of the emergence of a diversified and expanded curatorial field, the intensified appeal to a wide spectrum of discursive practices as artistic and curatorial métier, and the

*30   Wilson, "Curatorial Moments and Discursive Turns," 208.

*31   A figure is an image that organizes thinking without the necessity of fixing or finalizing conceptual definition. Figuration here refers to a way of thinking that does not proceed by delimiting conceptual boundaries to a term, as for example by specifying criteria of inclusion/exclusion with respect to a categorical distinction. The contrast here is between (i) a conceptual mode of thinking—using the discursive as a categorical term to make an absolute distinction between the discursive and the nondiscursive, or to posit a fundamental property held in common by all things that are properly designated as discursive; and (ii) a figurative mode of thinking— using descriptions of concrete instances as a way to think the character of the discursive by attending to multiple and diverse aspects of the sociomaterial situatedness and qualia of language events. In practice these modes are integral to the process of thinking, but the contrast between the two can be useful, as it hopefully is here.

                                                                       Mick Wilson

ambivalent valuation of the discursive that accompanied these.

The preliminary figuring of the discursive in this section leads on to an exploration of the theme of curating and the curatorial in the next section. We have already encountered one of the ways in which the term curating is generally used, in the case of the "curated conversation" of the anthropologists discussed above. There the term is employed to indicate operations of selecting, staging, editing, and prioritization. However, we will see that this sense of the term is not the currently preferred one within the professional field. Curating in itself is of course one of those spaces where the unresolved questions of the work of language are keenly felt and where rhetorical framing of projects is often exquisitely cultivated. This is clearly attested to by the last two decades of work on the "curating/the curatorial" couplet. In the next sections, I will both propose a way of analyzing how this couplet acts in regards to the discursive and address the question of what language does by itemizing some different theorizations of the couplet and their rhetorical effects.

CURATING/
THE CURATORIAL

> I find myself speaking with others
> about the curatorial, writing when
> asked about the curatorial, and reading
> other people's writing about what the
> curatorial "is" and what the curatorial
> "is not." I cannot help wondering: how
> did we get here? How did we get to
> a place where the curatorial matters
> so much? Does it matter? How? To
> whom? Is the curatorial a condition?
> A device? Is it a field or subject? How
> does it claim certain conventions
> around curating, while also claiming
> that one operates differently through
> the curatorial?[32]

As Sarah Pierce notes here, the twin construction of "curating/the curatorial" is by now a well-rehearsed and varied script. It has been proposed and problematized by several key protagonists within the field, including, in addition to Pierce, Beatrice von Bismarck, Charles Esche, Maria Lind, Jean-Paul Martinon, Paul O'Neill, Bonaventure Soh Bejeng Ndikung, and Irit Rogoff, among many others.[33] This rhetorical strategy has multiplied in diverse purposes, usages, and stakes over the last two decades. The 2013 book *The Curatorial: A Philosophy of Curating*, from which the Pierce citation is taken,

*32   Sarah Pierce, "The Simple Operator," in *The Curatorial: A Philosophy of Curating*, ed. Jean-Paul Martinon (London: Bloomsbury, 2014), 97.

*33   For an interesting set of competing accounts of curating/ the curatorial, see the forthcoming first issue of the new online journal *The Curatorial*.

provides what is perhaps the richest variety of glosses and expansions on the "curating/the curatorial" couplet gathered in one place. In their preface to the anthology, Martinon and Rogoff locate it within a desire to "talk about curating" that also includes a wish to talk about "the knowledges" curating "produces" and the "sociabilities, collectivities and convivialities" of curating. They institutionally inscribe this framework into "a space of gathering, a practice-led PhD program in 2006 called Curatorial/Knowledge," an institutional locus attached to the book.[34]

In what has become, alongside Lind's text cited above, one of the most frequently cited texts in the discussion to date,[35] Martinon and Rogoff write: "To drive home a distinction between 'curating' and 'the curatorial' means to emphasize a shift from the staging of the event to the actual event itself: its enactment, dramatization and performance."[36] In a passage repeatedly cited by other writers on the topic, they assert that:

*34   Jean-Paul Martinon and Irit Rogoff, "Preface," in *The Curatorial: A Philosophy of Curating*, ed. Jean-Paul Martinon (London: Bloomsbury, 2014), viii.

*35   See for example: Soh Bejeng Ndikung, "Detecting / Distilling Care in Curating / the Curatorial," in *Not Going It Alone: Collective Curatorial Curating*, ed. Paul O'Neill, Gerrie van Noor, and Elizabeth Larison (New York: apexart, 2024), 42; O'Neill, "Exhibitions as Curatorial Readymade Forms of Escape," in *Curating after the Global: Roadmaps for the Present*, eds. Paul O'Neill, Simon Sheikh, Gerrie van Noor, and Mick Wilson (Cambridge, MA: MIT Press, 2019), 500-501; and Carolina Rito and Bill Balaskas "Introduction," in *Institution as Praxis: New Curatorial Directions for Collaborative Research*, ed. Rito and Balaskas (Berlin: Sternberg, 2020), 15.

*36   Martinon and Rogoff, "Preface," ix.

                                          Mick Wilson

> If "curating" is a gamut of professional practices that had to do with setting up exhibitions and other modes of display, then "the curatorial" operates at a very different level: it explores all that takes place on the stage set-up, both intentionally and unintentionally, by the curator and views it as an event of knowledge.[37]

Later in the book, Martinon emphasizes the disruptive role of "the event" of the curatorial: "The curatorial is a disruptive activity. It disrupts received knowledge... the curatorial is a disruptive generosity." It "can never be properly translated into language" and it "gives the slip to the economy of received and exchanged knowledge."[38]

Doreen Mende's pithy essay in the same volume plays with the "curating/the curatorial" distinction not as a dichotomy, but rather as an aporia and a matter of poesis, through the use of three figures: "the blind spot," "inhibiting," and "the symptom."[39] The first of these invokes the junction between the optical nerve and the retina, where light does not register: "This blind spot is what throws us into the arena of the curatorial, this a-synchronous world full of ambivalences. While curating helps us

*37   Martinon and Rogoff, "Preface," ix.

*38   Jean-Paul Martinon, "Theses in the Philosophy of Curating," in *The Curatorial: A Philosophy of Curating*, ed. Jean-Paul Martinon (London: Bloomsbury, 2014), 26.

*39   Doreen Mende, "Three Short Takes on the Curatorial," in *The Curatorial: A Philosophy of Curating*, ed. Jean-Paul Martinon (London: Bloomsbury, 2014), 105–8.

to programme located public events, the blinding effect of the blind spot makes us enter a place (the curatorial) where we lose control and orientation."[40] Mende proposes a paradoxical complementarity between "curating" and "the curatorial": "This blinding 'moment' cannot be reified, replaced, or represented because, in the moment of exposure, it escapes the creative action of exposing. It is a moment in which 'exhibiting' is not there yet, but is in the process of being constituted."[41]

Mende's figurative account of the curatorial resonates with Paul O'Neill's thesis on "exhibitions as curatorial readymade forms of escape," where he notes that "certain articulations of the curatorial have identified a strand of practice that seeks to resist categorical resolution, preferring to function… as a constellation of activities that do not wish to fully reveal themselves."[42] Often, as with Rogoff, Martinon, and also Mende, "curating/the curatorial" is deployed as a paradoxical, determinately elusive, and dialectically fugitive rhetorical device, in the kind of terminological construction familiar from discourses on the aesthetic and the affective. The curatorial might then be seen as an attempt to reconstruct terms of aesthetic analysis with a focus on the networked assemblage of artistic works rather than on any (putative) self-sufficiency of the work of art, with a focus on aesthesis rather than on

*40   Mende, "Three Short Takes on the Curatorial," 105.

*41   Mende, "Three Short Takes on the Curatorial," 106.

*42   O'Neill, "Exhibitions as Curatorial Readymade Forms of Escape," 502.

                                              Mick Wilson

moments of aesthetic judgement as such.[43]

There is an emphatic reflexivity and ambivalence in these various addresses to "curating/the curatorial." They announce both a desire to "talk about curating" and a sense of language as a horizon that cannot fully access this desire or render "translatable" the occasion of "the curatorial," which nonetheless incites discourse. The impulse to talk about the curatorial and situate discursivity as one of its dimensions clashes, at the same time, with the impulse to declare the inadequacy of language to disclose it.

Sometimes the curatorial is posited in contrast or in opposition to curating, as in Lind's and Martinon's texts. Sometimes it is posited in contrast to the exhibition and the discrete operations of producing a show: "the curatorial as a cultural practice that goes well beyond the mere organizing of exhibitions."[44] However, more often "the curatorial" is proposed not as antithetical to, nor fully

*43   The relationship between aesthetics and discursivity is fundamentally contested and overlaps with the way in which the role of judgement in aesthetic experience is also contested. As Sianne Ngai has argued, "The centrality of judgment to aesthetic experience remains controversial. For Kant, Clement Greenberg, and others, it seems like there can be no such thing as an aesthetic experience without judgment, while Nietzsche and others suggest the contrary. I think the former camp is ultimately right on this, which is why I treat aesthetic categories as both discursive evaluations ('cute' as something we say, a very particular way of communicating a very particular kind of pleasure) and as objective styles (cuteness as a commodity aesthetic, as a sensuous/formal quality of objects), and try to pay close attention to the relation between them." See Adam Jasper and Sianne Ngai, "Our Aesthetic Categories: An Interview with Sianne Ngai," *Cabinet* 43 (2011), https://www.cabinetmagazine.org/issues/43/jasper_ngai.php.

segregable from, curating, but rather as an integrally related though differentiated—indeed, sometimes disidentified—moment, surplus, or even preemption of curating practice.[45]

Sarah Pierce elegantly deflates this recurrent preoccupation with the relation between the two terms: "We can acknowledge that the curatorial 'normally' relates to curating. Let us say, for now, contiguity exists, and that is all."[46] Pierce describes this as a "partly tactical" move "to disengage the curatorial from the professional work of the curator" so that the curatorial can be approached without continually returning "to define the curatorial through the systems and structures of curating as they exist." Pierce writes that this also has the advantage of not constraining the discussion of curatorial "ways of producing" as necessarily always pivoting on the agency of "a curator." Paul O'Neill, writing a few years later, and summarizing the growing range of glosses on "the curatorial," notes that "these nuanced definitions of 'the curatorial' may be read as forms of resistance to the primacy of the practice of curating." He argues, however, that "this is not the primary objective of the curatorial

*44   Nora Sternfeld and Luisa Ziaja, "What Comes After the Show? On Post-Representational Curating," *Talking about Exhibition: An Anthology*, ed. Maria Hussakowska (Krakow: Jagiellonian University, 2012), 127.

*45   In an earlier draft I wrote of a "terminological distinction" between these. However, it seems clear that what is proposed with these two constructs is not a categorical distinction nor dichotomy but rather a complementarity, not a contrastive difference but rather one of register.

*46   Sarah Pierce, "The Simple Operator," 100.

                                                    Mick Wilson

which prioritizes a type of working with others within a temporary space of cooperation, coproduction, and discursivity that allows ideas to emerge in the process of doing and speaking together."[47]

In these different contributions we return upon themes of the discursive and of speaking together as outlined in the introduction. We shuttle back and forth between discursive practices positioned as immanent to the field of curating and discursive practices as attempts at constituting the field, and we encounter the different ways in which an incitement to discourse resonates across all these instances. One way of reading the discussion of curating/the curatorial is as a moment of self-conscious field formation, especially in the trading zone between universities and museums or between academic institutions and artistic frameworks.[48] Across this typology of sites—trading zones, academic settings, artistic scenes—questions of how to cope with different regimes of discursive practice and which discursive practices are

*47   O'Neill, "Exhibitions as Curatorial Readymade Forms of Escape," 501.

*48   Trading zone is a term introduced by Peter Galison in his *Image and Logic: A Material Culture of Microphysics*, (Chicago: University of Chicago Press, 1979) to describe the intersection arenas of physics as sites where groups from different technical traditions—experimentalists, instrument-makers, theorists—are called upon to collaborate within the laboratory. It is a concept that has been anchored in Science and Technology Studies for some time, and has been given wider currency across other disciplines in recent decades as a metaphor of encounter across language domains, where coping strategies emerge to achieve functional forms of mutual intelligibility but where there is no guarantee of a symmetric, shared ontology among those interacting in the trading zone.

appropriate are already intensely activated.

I propose a further dimension of usage to unpack, which is the sense of curating as selection and prioritization. A noteworthy shift in the circulation of the term "curating" (and the adjectival form of "curatorial") is the generalized transfer of "curating" to name activities beyond the contemporary art and museum sectors that are connected to content selection. In spring 2020, the *New York Times* carried a short article under the headline "Everyone's a Curator Now: When Everything Is 'Curated,' What Does the Word Even Mean?" The article points to the widespread use of curating as a fashionable term: "It's mainstream jargon now... It's used because it sounds fashionable. It sounds like it's for... the aesthetically conscious."[49] It is also noteworthy that these adopted usages of "curating" are most strongly correlated with the notions of selecting, of "gatekeeping," and the power of legitimization. These themes are much less prominent within the reflexive discourse of curating itself. Indeed, it seems that the couplet "curating/the curatorial" does a significant amount of work in building some

*49   Lou Stoppard, "Everyone's a Curator Now: When Everything Is 'Curated,' What Does the Word Even Mean?" The New York Times, March 3, 2020, https://www.nytimes.com/2020/03/03/style/curate-buzzword.html. For a more considered reading of this development, see Vipash Purichanont's doctoral dissertation, *Curation of the Self: Genealogy of Curatorial Practice and Neoliberal Subjectivation* (Goldsmiths College, 2018), where he has mapped the ways in which the terms "curating" and "curator" have been adopted across the "creative economy," operating as part of a wider power apparatus not restricted to contemporary art and museology and analyzing this in terms of an apparatus of neoliberal subject formation.

                                                        Mick Wilson

distance between professional discursive practices and this popularized vernacular of curating as content selection and gatekeeping.[50] This treatment of the couplet both indicates the centrality of discursive production in constituting the field and also unsettles any simple division between discourse on curatorial practice and discourse *as* curatorial practice.

*50   Interestingly, the term curating has been taken up in communications and media studies in ways specifically related to the established idea of "gatekeeping." This can be seen, for example, in the analysis of "curated flows" that "considers the roles of journalistic actors in content production and dissemination (gatekeeping) alongside four additional sets of curating actors: individual media consumers themselves; social others embedded in online and offline networks; strategic communicators; and algorithms designed to shape the discovery and presentation of content in many digital contexts." Kjerstin Thorson and Chris Wells, "How Gatekeeping Still Matters: Understanding Media Effects in an Era of Curated Flows," in *Gatekeeping in Transition*, ed. Tim P. Vos and François Heinderyckx (London: Routledge, 2015), 25–44. A similar usage is to be seen by other media scholars: "Critics and curators generate value for those who are creating material and perhaps for one another. Critics provide ideas about which content to value, and curators provide critics with easy access to the texts being examined." Henry Jenkins, Sam Ford, and Joshua Green, *Spreadable Media: Creating Value and Meaning in a Networked Culture* (New York University Press, 2013), 157–8. See also Sanna Malinen, "The Owners of Information: Content Curation Practices of Middle-Level Gatekeepers in Political Facebook Groups," *New Media & Society* 26, no.1 (2021): 495–512.

THE DISCURSIVE RETURNS

In both sections two and three, I have used the phrasing "discursive practices" to cover many different sources. However, in doing so I have risked repeating the error, identified in the earlier work on this topic, of not attending sufficiently to the differences between very diverse modalities, formats, and genres: speaking, writing, discussing, debating, conversing, and so forth. Here it might be helpful to revisit the anecdotes of conversational encounter provided in section two. These scenes figure the sociomaterial density of concrete instances of discursive interaction in the absence of both a fully resolved schema of genres and modes and a well-rehearsed theory of language as such. It has been argued that under such conditions it is still possible to explore discursive practices by drawing upon broadly rhetorical analyses. And it is within this framework that the different kinds of work the couplet "curating/the curatorial" is doing, or attempting to do, across these different instances can be unpacked.

When we consider the work that the couplet does rhetorically, we attend provisionally to the communicative functions and the situational effects of the use of this couplet produces, rather than simply reading along the axis of word meaning. Taking this approach, we can see "curating/the curatorial" operating as a descriptor. Practitioners construct the term in an effort to disclose what it is they are doing, what matters in their work, and how it comes to matter.[51] We can also see "curating/the curatorial" as an evaluator, a normative term elaborated by practitioners in their attempt to indicate what should be done within the practice. We can also see it as an enactor, a performative term that (at least in part) is doing what it describes and names, a way of speaking that reframes and reorients the attention brought to bear within the unfolding of the practice.[52] It is proposed that part of this move entails deprioritizing curating's selective and gatekeeping connotations, which characterize the term's usage in other settings such as popular culture and in other disciplines.

Approaching the term in this way—as descriptor, as evaluator, as enactor—means (as indicated above) that we are not seeking to finalize a definition but rather understand instrumental aspects of the term across multiple utterance formats, modes, and genres. This instrumental aspect is not only a matter of how the term is deployed; it also concerns the practical, conceptual, and professional purposes, functions, and persuasive effects that the term accomplishes in different scenarios. Furthermore, it seems that the relatively unfixed semantic drive of the term—its slipperiness,

*51   For example, Carolina Cerón proposes to apply the term "the curatorial" to Gustavo Zalamea's practice, which "arguably explored the notion of the curatorial before it was identified" in a move that proposes "to dilute the limits that operate within the curatorial paradigm in the global north." See Carolina Cerón, "All Those Things Are Also Ours: De lo Blando en lo Curatorial," in *Institution as Praxis: New Curatorial Directions for Collaborative Research*, ed. Rito and Balaskas (Berlin: Sternberg, 2020), 77.

*52   The theory of performatives is familiar not only in the philosophy of language but across a broad swathe of cultural theory and criticism. See John L. Austin, *How to Do Things With Words* (Cambridge, MA: Harvard University Press, 1962).

                                    Mick Wilson

its wish not to fully reveal itself, its insistence on untranslatable moments—is integral to its utility in this regard. If its instrumental use was exclusively or primarily normative or descriptive, it would presumably be better accomplished by a term that effected a more precise cut or determinate category. A certain semantic openness, an unsettled quality of meaning, seems more useful where the speaker-writer's purpose is to disclose experiential, processual, and conceptual unsettledness, to indicate inchoate sensing, emergent thinking, or ontological indeterminacy.

To some, this term's unfixity might make it seem obscurantist, unwarranted, or empty.[53] In a recent contribution, explicitly addressing this wish to evade fixity, Bonaventura Soh Bejeng Ndikung problematizes the tendency of both "curating" and "the curatorial" to produce stasis in the practices nominated by these terms, and to restrict the dynamic, processual aspects that are for him paramount: "I am interested in thinking about curating in a state of perpetual change."[54] Using an analogy with the debates on créolité and creolization, and using the figure of marronage, he proposes "curatorialization" as a term to effect this evasion of fixity.[55]

> What I am proposing is that besides
> moving from the act of just displaying/

*53   Soh Bejeng Ndikung writes of "an era in which curating has come to mean everything and nothing." See "Detecting / Distilling Care in Curating / the Curatorial," 42.

*54   Ndikung, "Detecting / Distilling Care in Curating / the Curatorial," 43.

staging (curating) to enacting, drama-
tizing, and performing (the curatorial),
curatorialization would also have to
mean employing other strategies
that open up cracks and caveats of
care that we may not have explored
until now, and that constantly adapt
themselves to the needs of the artists,
the art and audiences, as well as times
and spaces—and most especially over
extended periods of time before and
beyond the exhibition itself.[56]

Interestingly, this appeal for unfixity and dynamism
is fused with a call to professional ethics. Soh
Bejeng Ndikung points out that: "Due to obvious

*55   "Créole" is a term coined in the 16th century by Spanish
and Portuguese colonizers. It was originally used to refer to
individuals born in the colonies who were of Portuguese, Spanish,
or African descent. In the late 17th century the French colonial
adventurer/explorer Michel Jajolet used the term Créole to refer
to a Portuguese-based language he heard spoken in Senegal.
Créole languages were initially defined as those which developed
on European plantation settlements throughout the 17th and 18th
centuries, combining elements of European and local languages.
The majority of these languages developed on the coasts of the
Atlantic and Indian oceans, but now the term is used to apply
to any language that emerges in the encounter of two or more
languages and operates as a "natural language," i.e., a language
that a child may potentially acquire as a first language. Créolité
became the name for a Caribbean literary movement that sought
to overcome the limitations of the earlier Négritude propounded
by Césaire, Senghor, and others. It has expanded as a concept
to address a wider process of cultural generativity that exceeds
the question of language alone. Créolité and créolization were
terms and ideas that have in some degree been embraced in
the contemporary art field, especially after their adoption as the
framework concepts for Platform 3 in Okwui Enzewor's 2002
Documenta11.

*56   Ndikung, "Detecting / Distilling Care in Curating / the
Curatorial," 44.

                                                   Mick Wilson

limits in time and funding, curators tend to delve rather superficially into certain subjects."[57] He illustrates this with reference to recurrent emails from "curator colleagues" who approach with questions along the lines of: "I am working on XYZ, please send me a list of African artists working on these issues." Soh Bejeng Ndikung's ethical intervention indicates another dimension of the situatedness of these utterances on "curating/the curatorial": the professional milieu within which these terms circulate. Soh Bejeng Ndikung, like other speakers and writers, the current included, through utterances on "curating/the curatorial," positions himself within a reputational economy and professional field. In this instance Soh Bejeng Ndikung presents himself as ethically reflective and responsible, connecting this to his own rhetorical care in further extending the couplet "curating/the curatorial" with his neologism of "curatorialization." This positioning is not quite the same as disclosing identity positions or other social coordinates. It may also be understood as a rhetorical move to indicate or produce the character or ethos of the speaker/writer. Ethos here is used to indicate how ways of speaking or writing both produce and draw upon the imagined qualities of the speaker/writer, making the empirical subject legible as an author.[58]

Gerrie van Noord, in her recent text "Beyond Hierarchy: Articulating Collaboration," cites Sara Ahmed's view that "refusal to enter the discourse as

*57 Ndikung, "Detecting / Distilling Care in Curating / the Curatorial," 46.

an empirical subject" can tend toward "a universalising mode of discourse… that negates the specificity of its own inscription."[59] This argument prompts van Noord to observe that "it is arguably precisely the tension between the generic and the specific that haunts so much curatorial literature."[60] This leads her to posit that there are "persistent contradictions between 'the doing' in artistic and curatorial practices and how they are described, inscribed and ultimately historicized."[61] Elsewhere, Paul O'Neill has underlined the repeated "contestation of the existence (and legitimacy) of a specifically curatorial field of praxis," pointing to various rehearsals of "curating/the curatorial" and indicating that these are often part of a "discursive field around curating "that is riddled with attempts to limit (or at least narrowly define) what curating should be… and… which bodies of knowledge shall have enduring consequence."[62]

*58   The term "ethos" in rhetorical analysis can be seen as overlapping in part with the term "position," as it has been used in positioning theory among various linguistically oriented social psychologists, such as Rom Harré. See Bronwyn Davies and Rom Harré, "Positioning and Personhood," in *Positioning Theory: Moral Contexts of International Action*, ed. Rom Harré and Luk van Langenhove (Oxford: Blackwell, 1999), 32–52.

*59   Gerrie van Noord, "Beyond Hierarchy: Articulating Collaboration," in *Not Going It Alone: Collective Curatorial Curating*, ed. Paul O'Neill, Gerrie van Noor, and Elizabeth Larison (New York: apexart, 2024), 120.

*60   Gerrie van Noord, "Beyond Hierarchy: Articulating Collaboration," 120.

*61   Gerrie van Noord, "Beyond Hierarchy: Articulating Collaboration," 121.

*62   O'Neill, "Exhibitions as Curatorial Readymade Forms of Escape," 500.

                                                   Mick Wilson

I cite Soh Bejeng Ndikung's, van Noord's, and O'Neill's different interventions here by way of drawing out another dimension of the usage of "curating/ the curatorial," which is the double action of constituting, within a scene of contested legitimation, both a specifically "curatorial" field of praxis and a specific practitioner within that field. In addition to the functioning of "curating/the curatorial" as descriptor, evaluator, and enactor, it has another functional affordance then as "positioner," as a producer of a specific professional positionality.[63]

In trying to map the usage and function of the "curating/the curatorial" couplet, we have been attending to the general terms of articulation of a practical field rather than to concrete instances of practice. This has been necessary in part because we are operating in the absence of a resolved theory of language and without a systemic construal of the discursive as such. It has also been necessary in part because the discursive operations around the constitution of the curatorial field have demonstrated a high degree of reflexive metalinguistic play and performativity. Although I have alluded to the sociomaterial density of the figures of conversation to avoid defaulting to some form of self-referential closure in "talk-about-talk," the reader may understandably long for some empirical instances

*63   I am using "positioning" here to indicate a type of deictic function. While deictic words typically invoke position with regard to a particular time, place, or person relative to the context of the utterance, I am suggesting here a kind of extended deixis that refers not to the spatiotemporal axes but rather to the socioprofessional standing of the speaker.

of the curatorial and the discursive in action. In the closing section of this essay there follows a short description of a concrete curatorial project and an artistic work that it engendered, both of which play across multiple registers of the discursive. This final anecdote expresses a potential opening within the space of the curatorial to explore the discursive beyond the inherited paradigms mandated by philosophy, linguistics, humanities scholarship, literary criticism, and rhetoric. This final scene may also be read as a counterpoint to the incitement to discourse described in Ray's account of the cultivation of the self-expressive individual in the early modern Salons. In this last scene, we encounter an attempt to attend to language's resistance to instrumental capture, echoing Abram's claim that we are "unable to circumscribe the whole of language."[64] Rather than an incitement to discourse as civilizing gesture, there is a different lilt to the scene of singing and a different grammar of call and response.

*64   David Abram, *The Spell of the Sensuous: Perception and Language in a More-than-Human World*, 52.

                                          Mick Wilson

TO SEMINAR

Is this a real site or an imaginary one? Neither. An institution is treated in the utopian mode: I outline a space and call it: seminar. It is quite true that the gathering in question is held weekly in Paris, i.e., here and now; but these adverbs are also those of fantasy. Thus, no guarantee of reality, but also nothing gratuitous about the anecdote. One might put things differently: that the (real) seminar is for me the object of a (minor) delirium, and that my relations with this object are, literally, amorous.[65]

In 2017, I was invited to participate in a project curated by Henk Slager at BAK Utrecht that took as its point of departure this citation from Roland Barthes and also its title: *To Seminar*.[66] The invitation was to join in a process of responding to this invocation of a space both discursive and amorous. The task was to construct something to be presented in the exhibition space, to join in a series of public events within the space of an exhibition and to contribute a

*65   Roland Barthes, *The Rustle of Language* (Berkeley and Los Angeles: University of California Press, 1989), 332.

*66   The exhibition took place from March 11 to May 21, 2017, and the publication *To Seminar*, edited by Henk Slager, was released by MetropolisM Books in August 2017. The participants in the project were Buse Aktaş, Tiong Ang, Şafak Çatalbaş, Jeremiah Day, Adnan Devran, Iris Ergül, İnci Eviner, René Francisco, Ola Hassanain, Sara van der Heide, Marijke Hoogenboom, Job Koelewijn, Jan Yongdeok Lim, Winston Nanlohy, Andrés Novo, Kristina Országhová, Sırma Öztaş, Sarah Pierce, Falke Pisano, Alejandro Ramirez, Vivian Sky Rehberg, Irit Rogoff, Heekyung Ryu, Ecem Sarıçayır, Margo Slomp, Marquard Smith, Camila Sposati, Jan Verwoert, Robert Wittendorp, Kitty Zijlmans, and Mick Wilson.

short text to a publication that would be produced in the wake of the exhibition. The project was framed as "evolving over time through a series of performative and discursive public meetings" that sought to "inquire into the practices of learning about, with, and through art."[67] Drawing upon Barthes, the proposition was that "[i]f, like Barthes' time of writing, ours is a present immersed in 'a certain apocalypse in culture,'" then the task is "to collectively think through and act out alternative imaginaries."[68] This instance of thinking and imagining otherwise is a sixth scenario of conversation and completes the set of concrete instances used in this essay.

Here, I wish to indicate schematically something of the dynamic and texture of this conversational encounter through a description of my participation. There were four aspects to this: there were several audio recordings of a song, "Dónal Óg," being sung in different styles and melodies that played erratically for several minutes, sounding out approximately every hour or so during the run of the exhibition. There was a small chapbook available in the exhibition space, copies of which were available for free to be taken by exhibition visitors. This small booklet informed on its opening pages that "Dónal Óg is the name of a song that is sung in Gaelic and in English. It is sung in different tunes, and it is sung with different words. It is sung under different titles.

*67   "To Seminar," bak, https://archive2.bakonline.org/program-item/instituting-otherwise/to-seminar/.

*68   "To Seminar," bak, https://archive2.bakonline.org/program-item/instituting-otherwise/to-seminar/.

                                                        Mick Wilson

It is also spoken, written and printed as a poem in both languages." This was followed by several versions in English and Gaelic of the song's lyrics and various short fragments on different aspects of the song and its performances. In the opening pages there is a short consideration of Dónal Óg's status as a linguistic object or discursive event.

> I refer to it, as "it," the song Dónal Óg.
> I tell people, the few who ask, that I am
> bringing it to To Seminar. However,
> I don't know if that is a correct thing
> to say. Barthes writes that "in the sem-
> inar… no discourse is sustained (but a
> text is sought)." Dónal Óg is not a text.
> The work here is not a reading. It is
> a relay of addresses.
> The song itemises and instantiates
> a series of calls, a sequence of direct
> and indirect hailings, in various forms,
> between animals, people, and things:
> "O lad…"; "in your name calling…";
> "I whistled and called you…"; "my moth-
> er ordered…"; "my mother will ask you
> to name your people." The song hails
> me because it moves from the crossing
> of water to the projection of utter loss.
> It calls. It transfers. It operates. It is
> a not a right thing.[69]

*69   Mick Wilson, *Dónal Óg (To Seminar)* (Gothenburg: Valand Academy, 2017), 7.

During the run of the exhibition, there was a series of public discussion events, including short presentations and exchanges, and at one of these I presented a short account of the research strand out of which "Dónal Óg" and other vocal works had emerged. The presentation entailed live vocalization and prerecorded material and was interrupted from time to time, as were the other participant presentations, by the intrusion of the exhibited audio track like a too-often repeated unfunny line in a dinner conversation. The opening theme of my presentation was the progressive removal of vernacular vocal music from the everyday spaces of colonial modernity—whistling, humming, singing, and so forth—and the imposition of a new aural regime. The fourth aspect of the contribution was a short text called "To Sing Song Seminar." In this way there was an attempt to weave multiple discursive practices through the site and apparatus of the exhibition (and elsewhere) by an artwork that had no single locus but that was distributed across multiple material instances.

Within the short essay published in the wake of the exhibition, there is a reading of the Barthes text against the grain of its voice. This is introduced through a short account of the transformation of the medieval practice of *disputatio* into the modern university seminar form. The turn to the seminar in the research training of nineteenth-century German universities is described with reference to the teaching of history and philology, noting that the seminar may have drawn something of its amicable

                                                                Mick Wilson

sociality and informality from the precedent of the literary salons. It is then proposed that the displacement of the late medieval and early modern traditions of *disputatio* by the nineteenth-century seminar format coincides with the emergence of textual production—as opposed to oral performance—as the primary form for demonstrating knowledge competency. On this basis the claim is then made that

> a particular economy of orality-textuality is activated within the seminar, that positions orality in the service of textual production, as the relay from text to text, that is somewhat different from the economies of orality-textuality that have been active at different times in the history of *disputatio*: oral performance as part end and part relay (switching multiply between moments of oral and textual production with dynamically shifting priorities and modes of relay) but not primarily as the relay from text to text.[70]

This rehearsal of the history of *disputatio* and seminar practices is not an exercise in nostalgia for an older discursive format. It is a device to bring into view other language practices, other discursive forms, other modalities of sociability, and other textures of conversational encounter.

*70   Mick Wilson, "To Sing Song Seminar," in *To Seminar*, ed. Henk Slager (Utrecht: MetropolisM Books, 2017), 59.

In opening this essay I asked how the incitement to discourse within contemporary curating and artistic practice might be understood in relation to the exhibition's and museum's historical civilizing imperatives. Rather than argue for a persistent incitement to discourse within the exhibitionary process that predates and informs the rise of the curatorial, I would like to gesture toward a different kind of continuity at work. In the liberal political imaginary, the idea of discursive exchange is recurrently upheld as intrinsically virtuous and civilizing, which is a pervasive feature of late modern liberal cultural policy.[71] Against this tendency, some—and I pointedly say some, not all nor even most—curatorial and artistic practices open up an exploration of discursivity that is not beholden to this credo. This alternate approach is alert to the ways in which discursive protocols constrain, subordinate, and discipline even as they also allow dissent, experimentation, and invention. Such curatorial experiments in the space of the discursive have the potential to contribute to a model of discursivity no longer predicated on Enlightenment ideals of reason or liberal figures of self-authoring possessive individuals, but rather upon ideas that proceed from other principles, conditions, and protocols of encounter and exchange.

*71   The valorization of discussion within policy discourse is pervasive, however, perhaps the most clear instances of this are to be seen in European policy frameworks that mandate "intercultural dialogue." See "The Role of Intercultural Dialogue in the EU Policy," *Journal of Intercultural Management* 2, no. 1 (2010): 78–88.

                                                                 Mick Wilson

One such format is the sing-song: a mode
of sociable gathering and an economy of affect
premised upon turn-taking in various forms of vocal
performance, although one typically not formatted
within the discipline of turn-taking at the polite table. The turn-taking of the sing-song is regulated by
protocols that also seek to reproduce and shore up
a given social order, as do the rules of polite conversation. However, they are routed through a different
genealogy, a different institutional trajectory, and,
when these intersect, murmers of another order
can become momentarily audible. In the modest
curatorial opening that *To Seminar* set up, the many
different modalities of the discursive were made
to sing together in overlapping turns through said
modalities' ad hoc orchestration. Considered in this
way, *To Seminar* partly qualifies the early formulation of the curatorial as "a way of linking objects,
images, processes, people, locations, histories, and
discourses in physical space" with which this essay
opened.

One of the possibilities of the curatorial is the
recalibration of discursivity: not as the movement
between subjects; not as analytic reason; not as a
reified entity that is assembled in concatenation
with other discrete entities—objects, images,
processes, people, locations, histories, et cetera;
not as simply a mode of inscription into a civilizing
project nor as a métier for virtuosity. This is the
discursive as both an agent of articulation, of linking
across disparate registers, and as a generativity, as
a vibrant, disruptive potential that, while subject to

reproductive regulation and operable in service of all manner of disciplinary and social stratification projects, always portends the possibility of an otherwise and elsewise being. This disruptive potential is fugitive and easily dissipated by the impulse to fix an event of language in its assigned place, to make it a matter of record. There is a risk that such an impulse also accompanies my rehearsal of conversational anecdotes and discursive scenes, as much as it might accompany their recording on some other inscription device. Taking account of this risk then, here, in this curatorial moment while spinning merrily in these discursive turns, I would like to propose the figure of the sing-song and invite you, dear reader, to sing along, in your own good time.

Biographies

Mick Wilson is an artist, educator and researcher based in Gothenburg and Dublin. He is currently Professor of Art, Director of Doctoral Studies at HDK-Valand, University of Gothenburg, and Co-Director of the Centre for Art and the Political Imaginary (CAPIm) a partnership between HDK-V Gothenburg and KKH Stockholm. Wilson has published extensively on contemporary curating. Some of the more distinct co-edited volumes include *Exhibitionary Acts of Political Imagination* (2021); *Curating after the Global* (2019); and *How Institutions Think: Between Contemporary Art and Curatorial Discourse* (2017), to name only a few.

Carolina Rito is a curator and researcher based in London. Rito is currently Professor of Creative Practice Research, at the Research Centre for Arts, Memory and Communities (CAMC), at Coventry University; and leads the centre's Critical Practices research strand and Curatorial Research cluster. Rito has published on curatorial practices and theory, *Institution as Praxis–New Curatorial Directions for Collaborative Research* (Sternberg, 2020), *Architectures of Education* (e-flux Architecture, 2020), and *FABRICATING PUBLICS: the dissemination of culture in the post-truth era* (Open Humanities Press, 2021).

Colophon

On the Curatorial, volume 1

Series editor
Carolina Rito

Copyediting
Jude Macannuco

Graphic design
Sofia Bresciani

Printing
Tallinna Raamatutrükikoja OÜ

© 2025 Floating Opera Press, Berlin, and the authors

Generous support provided by

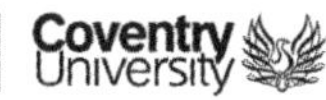

In collaboration with
Expanded Artistic Research Network

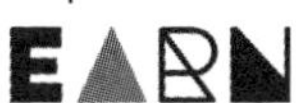

Published by:
Floating Opera Press
Hasenheide 9
10967 Berlin
www.floatingoperapress.com

ISBN 978-3-9826683-0-7

The idea of "the curatorial" arose in the mid-2000s
after a short but intense debate about what it means
to curate beyond exhibitions. The books in the
On the Curatorial series look at the consequences
of that discussion and ask: Do we need different
curatorial tools to engage with deepening social,
political, and ecological crises? The series allows
earlier participants in the debate to reflect on how
their concepts and practices have changed, while
younger generations of curators explore the ongoing
need for new conceptual approaches to curation.

Discourse has always played a central role in
exhibition-making, from wall texts and catalogues
to the discussions surrounding exhibitions.
In *On Discourse and the Curatorial*, Mick Wilson
examines the ongoing "incitement to discourse"
in the curatorial field and how it continues to shape
contemporary curatorial practices.

FLOATING OPERA PRESS

ISBN 978-3-9826683-0-7

9 783982 668307